MICHAEL COOPER

Discovering Farmhouse Cheese

SHIRE PUBLICATIONS LTD

Contents

ACKNOWLEDGEMENTS

The author gratefully acknowledges: his wife, Sue, without whose patience this book would not have been written; Martyn Brown of the Somerset Rural Life Museum, without whose encouragement this book might never have been written; Messrs H. and J. Green of Mulberry Farm, West Pennard, Glastonbury, and Mrs Hawkins, also of West Pennard; the Federations' Farmhouse English Cheese Information Office, 16 Bolton Street, London W1Y 8HX; Mr H. R. Cornwell, Cheese Executive, English Country Cheese Council.

Cover design and line illustrations by the author.

Printed in Great Britain by C. I. Thomas & Sons (Haverfordwest) Ltd, Press Buildings, Merlins Bridge, Haverfordwest.

1. The history of cheesemaking in England

The basic process of cheesemaking is the separation of milk into curds and whey and the treatment of these curds to preserve them as cheese, which can be eaten at a later date. So milk, a food that does not keep long, is made into a product that can be easily stored, transported and kept. In the past cheese provided a fresh dairy food supplying the goodness of milk when milk was no longer available, in the winter months.

Cheese has certainly been made in England since Roman times, if not longer, and the chief milk animal, until the sixteenth century, was the sheep. Palladius in his treatise on agriculture described precisely the methods used in Roman Britain; he detailed the use of rennet and other coagulants such as the milk of fig trees or teasel flowers. In 1208 cheese was recorded as being sold at seven shillings a 'pondus', a pondus being 42lb (19kg). Even in those days the food market suffered from rising prices and a pondus had risen to thirteen shillings and fourpence by 1299. Unlike today, prices occasionally came down as well and a pondus was nine shillings by 1304.

Large tracts of agricultural land were under monastic control during the middle ages and the self-sufficient skills developed in the monasteries included cheesemaking. Local labour was employed on the farm and in the dairy: at least one prior thought that the comely appearance of the dairymaids might have been even more popular than the cheese and instructed that only 'old and ill-favoured' females should be employed 'within the monastic boundaries'.

The recipes of certain cheeses were almost confined to these religious houses. The Cistercian monks of Jervaulx Abbey are said to have brought their famous, probably Norman, recipe to Wensleydale in North Yorkshire and to have made the cheese there exclusively until Henry VIII sacked their property in 1536. Thereafter the cheese was made in local dairies. As time went on, more cheese found its way into the markets and in the seventeenth century certain people, mainly women, were licensed to trade in cheese in specific counties. These women, known as 'badgers', became the first wholesalers of cheese and butter, travelling from town to town with their 'three horses, mares or geldings', as their licence permitted. This was the origin of the system whereby cheese factors were responsible for buying and selling most of the dairy farmers' produce.

The best cheeses were said to come from Cheddar, Cheshire, Salop, Suffolk and Essex. In 1533 Henry VIII had received a gift of six Suffolk cheeses from Lady Calthrop. It is unlikely, though, that he would ever have been given a Kent cheese as they were notorious for being the 'very worst'. The royal table was probably

3

heavy with cheese as the trade increased and more was made. The poor farmworker or cottager saw little of this sort of cheese: traditionally he made 'common cheese', from the skimmed milk left from buttermaking, which quickly turned hard and crumbly. When common grazing became scarce, as enclosures increased and his cow had no pasture, expensive cheese often ceased to be part of his diet.

Indeed, even prosperous people were concerned about the price of Cheddar and in 1661 Samuel Pepys, his wife and household were most 'vexed' at trying to make do with Suffolk cheese in attempts to curb their extravagance of taste.

As the population and prosperity of England increased so did the demand for cheese in the newly wealthy cities. Cheesemongers built warehouses around the country, transporting their goods by road and water. Buying cheese in the poorer agricultural counties of the west and north and selling it in London and abroad for the tables of the rich, they made a handsome profit. Cheese merchants became wealthy and influential men. By the end of the seventeenth century the demand was such that small farms and entire villages joined together in cooperatives to supply this new market.

Daniel Defoe wrote of the village of Cheddar and its cheese in *A Tour through the Whole Island of Great Britain* in 1724-6: 'In the low country, on the other side Mendip Hills, lies Cheddar, a village pleasantly situated under the very ridge of the mountains; before the village is a large green or common, a piece of ground in which the whole herd of cows belonging to the town do feed; the ground is exceeding rich, and as the whole village are cowkeepers, they take care to keep up the goodness of the soil by agreeing to lay on large quantities of dung for manuring and enriching the land. The milk of all the town cows is brought together every day in a common room, where persons appointed, or trusted for the management, measure every man's quantity and set it down in a book; when quantities are adjusted, the milk is put together, and every meal's milk makes one cheese, and no more; so that the cheese is bigger or less, as the cows yield more, or less, milk. By this method, the goodness of the cheese is preserved and, without all dispute, it is the best cheese that England affords, if not that the whole world affords.'

Two or three thousand tons of cheese a year were now being sent to London to feed the half million or so people who lived there; fresh milk was scarce and cheese provided a useful part of their diet. With almost a monopoly by the 1760s, the cheesemongers were the subject of much criticism by the poor farmer, who had a cash-flow problem as he had to store the cheese for months, suffered from any loss in its weight and had extra work while he waited for the cheesemongers or factors to accept it when they were ready.

Local markets and fairs such as Chippenham, Bridgwater and Marlborough were famous for their cheese. One great cheese fair was held every September at Atherstone on Stour in Warwickshire where factors bought much of the produce and rushed it to Stourbridge fair, which lasted longer, and gained a quick profit there. Regulations had been introduced earlier to prevent dealers buying and selling the same cheese on the same day at the same fair, such was the wheeling and dealing of the market place.

Cheddar cheese, already the most famous, had many competitors by now: Wiltshire and Gloucestershire cheeses were made by the thousands of tons in the late eighteenth century. Some Dorset cheeses were sold as Bridgwater cheese; other areas, too, imitated the better-known kinds and none paid much attention to correct trade descriptions.

From cows such as the Longhorn, which can be traced back to the iron age, the farmer was now getting 4 to 5 cwt (200-250kg) of cheese a year. Cheese was not the only product, however: the whey butter and the calves were also included in the balance sheet. But out of this the dairymaid's wages of £3 to £4 a year would have to be paid — her reward for getting up at dawn and milking her cows before starting work in the cheeseroom; this took most of the day and even then she had not finished — the storeroom work that followed would have been enough to tire many a man today, for it was no light task turning and cleaning the heavy cheeses, which needed constant attention. According to an old Somerset adage

'If you'll have a good cheese and have'n old
You must turn'n seven times before's cold.'

Often the cheeses were stored on sheaves of stinging nettles, which were said to aid their maturing, and branches of elder had to be cut and placed in the stores to ward off flies and evil spirits.

Presumably careless storage or too much acidity produced the first blue cheeses. These were first sought after during the eighteenth century and farmers soon learnt to produce the conditions that encouraged the growth of the blue mould that commanded such a premium. The famous Stilton cheese, selling at two shillings and sixpence a pound, was certainly a luxury and the Dorset Blue or Blue Vinny was made in many a dairy in the Dorchester area.

The eighteenth century saw a more organised approach to farming, pioneered by the model farms and agricultural reformers such as Arthur Young (1741-1820) and William Cobbett (1763-1835). Their many papers and books on all aspects of agriculture led to the changes that were to follow over the next hundred years. Agricultural societies were very active in this new movement; the Bath and West Society opened its first laboratory in 1806. The Board of Agriculture was formed in 1792 and undertook a survey of all counties; great improvements were made in the feeding of cattle, especially in the winter months, and milk yields rose in general.

The new methods and systems suggested by the zealous reformers did not meet with instant and absolute approval. The hard-working dairymaids often viewed the new ideas with suspicion. The advice of mere men in what they considered their domain and the suggestion that their proudly guarded recipes, handed down from mother to daughter, needed improvement could not have been to their liking. Many of them were now earning £6 a year and some were quite famed for their cheese and proud of their reputation, though there are accounts that the dairymaids of Norfolk were considered to 'have little skill', their cheeses often being 'bags of maggots'.

The mechanisation of the industrial revolution did little at first to make the dairymaid's job any easier. She slowly discarded some of her wooden utensils for the new metal ones, but it was not until tinned containers became available that they were readily accepted, although the effect of the repeated use of the wooden ones on the milk had long been suspected. Milk dishes of various designs may still be seen in museums. Of the pottery ones the stoutest was probably the white Wedgwood-ware dish with a lip at one end. There was also a very graceful light-green glass dish manufactured by a certain Mr Pellet of London. Both these dishes were easily cleaned and easily broken, unlike the sturdy wooden dishes cooper-made of oak staves bound with iron hoops.

The dairy building itself was usually on the north side of the farmhouse, where it was coolest. Its lattice windows were often provided with shutters to regulate the temperature a little. So important were these windows that they were freed from the

Fig. 1. Milk dishes c. 1800: (top left) pottery; (bottom left) glass; (right) wooden.

Fig. 2. Cutting the curd in a copper cheese vat, showing the overhead heater.

window tax of 1808-51; Section 13 of the Act exempted all such windows provided that they were labelled, with a sign above, DAIRY or CHEESE ROOM in Roman letters, which may still be seen on some dairy buildings today. Rooms so labelled had to be used for that purpose and were 'not to be slept in'.

Inside the dairy, the cheese tub itself was usually made of copper, now tinned on the inside and standing on a wooden base that could be tilted with a lever to drain off the whey through a tap at the base of the side. An improvement on this was the jacketed tub, connected to one of the new boilers, which allowed steam to circulate around it in water. If the steam had been applied directly to the container it would have cooked the curd to the sides. Another system, preferred by many for some time, was the overhead heater; by this method a little milk or whey could be removed from the tub to a smaller tub above and heated separately before being returned to the first tub, thus raising the temperature of the whole.

These shining copper tubs were later replaced by oblong jacketed vats containing from 40 to 600 gallons (182 to 2728 litres). These were much easier to work and, as well as holding larger quantities of milk, had other advantages. Milk could be cooled in them overnight by circulating cold water in the jacket and the entire job of cheesemaking could be performed in the vat instead of removing the curd to a separate cooler, as was often necessary. Even during this modernisation, attempts were made to retain the rural atmosphere of the dairy, for the new vats were carefully painted in a simulated wood-grain finish on the outside. These improvements in turn gave way to the vast stainless steel vats of today with their mechanical knives and stirrers that can deal with 3000 gallons (13,638 litres) of milk at a time.

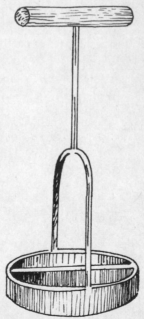

Fig. 3. Curd knife, c. 1800

Fig. 4. Wooden-handled brass curd breaker.

The milk was filtered through a fine-meshed strainer hanging from the side of the tub. This primitive cleaning of the milk has now been replaced by the pasteurising equipment which ensures bacteria-free milk of a constant quality. This was yet another step strongly resisted in many areas where it was thought that flavour might suffer through pasteurisation.

Rennet was added to the milk in the tub, causing it to coagulate, and the next step was to cut the curd. For this, new curd knives have replaced the old curd breaker and curd cutter. The curd breaker is one of the more attractive dairy bygones with its long wooden handle and brass-framed grid of wires. It was still useful for stirring in the old round tubs, but unless the wire and edges were well maintained it tended to smash the curd rather than cut it, resulting in the loss of valuable fat. The old curd cutter consisted of a bisected iron ring attached to a wooden handle above. Designed to be used with the oblong vat, the new knives were made up from a large grid of blades in a frame which could be worked up, down and across the coagulated curd, the many thin strips of tinned steel cutting the curd into regular pieces with little loss of fat or curd. These new cutters were known as the American Curd Knife and Pond's Curd Knife (which had diagonal blades). Pond's were makers of dairy equipment in Blandford Forum, Dorset.

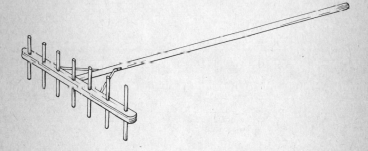

Fig. 5. Wooden curd rake.

9

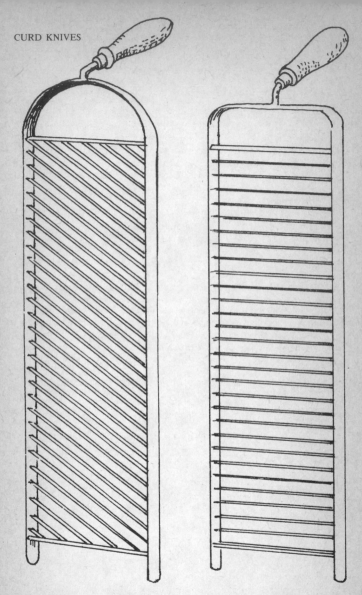

Fig. 6. Curd knives: (left) Pond's curd knife; (right) American curd knife.

Another bygone from the dairy is the curd rake, which was used, after the coagulated curd had been cut, to stir it during scalding and to settle or 'pitch' it afterwards. Made from a light wood, it was like a hay rake except that the teeth extended on either side of the blade. Used in oblong vats, it has generally been superseded by stainless steel rakes and mechanical agitators.

All this equipment required daily cleaning and scrubbing out, a hard task without modern detergents and chemical cleaners, but even these new aids need to be used correctly. Recently a Somerset farmer was heard to remark that the cheese vat should be scrubbed out 'the way the sun goes round'; it being considered very unlucky to pass a cider mug in an anticlockwise direction, he applied the same rule to other tasks.

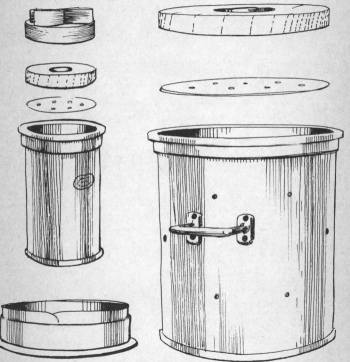

Fig. 7. Moulds and followers like these have been in use for the last century: (top left) truckle mould; (bottom left) Caerphilly mould; (right) 60 lb (27 kg) mould.

After scalding and pitching, the curd had to be passed through a mill, another of the newer features of the dairy, first introduced in the 1780s to help in the work of breaking up the curd, which had in the past been done by hand. The first mill consisted of two rollers about 6 inches (153mm) wide and 15 inches (380mm) long. The first roller had inch-long (25mm) spikes sticking out and the second a number of studs which ground the curd that had been shredded by the first roller. Curd was fed by hand through a wooden hopper above the rollers, which were turned by a large handle at the side. The present-day peg mill, used to grind cheese such as Double Gloucester, is still of basically the same design but made in stainless steel and powered by an electric motor.

The ground curd was then packed into moulds, sometimes called *vats* or *chessets*. The smaller moulds were often made from a single piece of wood, usually elm, which endures moisture well. Larger moulds, up to 18 inches (457mm) high, were made from

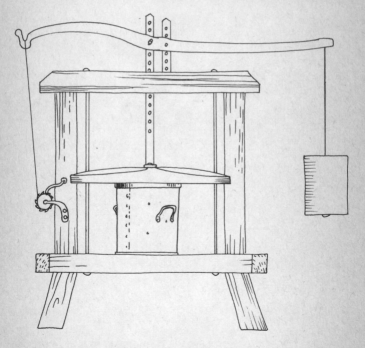

Fig. 8. Wooden cheese press, c. 1800, in the Somerset Rural Life Museum.

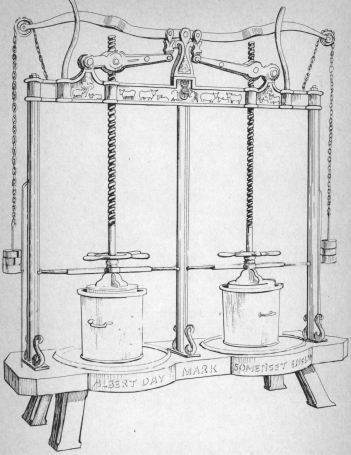

Fig. 9. Cast-iron cheese press, 1869, in the Somerset Rural Life Museum.

staves bound round with hoops of wood or later iron. Cheese requiring little pressure could be made in a mould that was a hoop alone, placed on a wooden cheeseboard. A wooden *sinker* was placed on top of a cheese that was to be pressed. It had to fit exactly to follow the cheese down into the mould as pressure was applied, letting no curd escape. Now known as *follower*, it may be made of metal, wood or polythene.

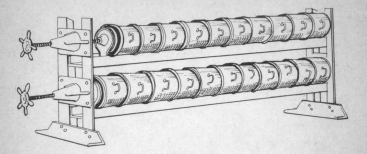

Fig. 10. Cast-iron gang press.

Before being placed in the press the cheese was pre-pressed for a few minutes to help the wet curd to bind and to expel the last of the whey. This was often the task of the plumpest dairymaid, leaning her full weight on the wooden lid. The earliest cheese presses consisted of just a heavy weight or stone placed directly on to the follower; later the stone was built into an iron or wooden frame, eventually lowered by an iron thread. These great stones, each weighing about 8 cwt (400 kg) can still occasionally be found in a farmyard or set into a nearby wall.

In the early nineteenth century the cast-iron press was invented, combining the use of a screw and lever. Two cheese moulds at a time, placed one above the other, could be subjected to a pressure of up to 1½ tons (1500 kg). As cheesemaking in factories got under

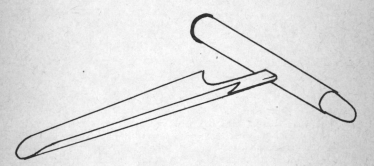

Fig. 11. Cheese iron or tester for taking samples for tasting.

way and farm production increased the gang press also became popular. A dozen or so large cheeses could be fitted into this, one pressing into another and tightened with a 'ship's wheel' at the end. This made it necessary to use a tapered cheese mould instead of the earlier straight-sided ones. Presses of this type are still in daily use in cheesemaking, though often with the addition of a hydraulic ram at the end.

Such was the equipment that was to be found in the dairy over the ages and may still be found — if not in the farmyard, then in antique shops or, more fittingly, in rural-life museums such as the Somerset Rural Life Museum in the Abbey Barn at Glastonbury or the James Countryside Museum at Bicton in Devon.

2. Cheddar cheese

The history of Cheddar

The most important English cheese is the famous Cheddar, which, as a farmhouse cheese, has been made for hundreds of years in the area between Cheddar, Wells and Shepton Mallet in Somerset and is now copied in factories the world over. It owes much of this success to Joseph Harding, who was born in 1805 at Marksbridge in Somerset.

He introduced a standard system of cheesemaking, eliminating many of the mistakes perpetuated by the handed-down recipes. The margins of error were reduced and by carefully following his rules a regular standard of results could be achieved. Harding's fame spread far and wide as cheeses made by his method won prizes at the agricultural shows. Delegations from Scotland, Scandinavia and later America came to study his system. His sons followed in his footsteps; one of them, Henry, went to Australia and introduced the Harding process there.

By the use of well-designed dairies and better standards of hygiene, he reduced the contamination which used to affect so many cheeses. He advocated the use of a commercially manufactured rennet which had until then been considered inferior by most cheesemakers, who preferred their own home-made, often tainted, product.

Under Harding's system the milk of the previous evening was heated and then mixed in the tub with the morning's milk to raise its temperature to 84F (29C). Rennet was then added, causing the milk to coagulate into a blancmange-like texture. After an hour this was broken up with a skimmer or curd breaker. The curds were thus separated from the whey, some of which was taken out. The remaining curd was cut further, into pieces the size of peas, over a period of fifteen minutes. The whey which had been removed was heated, then returned to the tub, raising the overall temperature to about 80F (27C). More whey was taken out, heated and returned, until the temperature was raised to 100F (38C) over a period of thirty minutes. Stirring with the skimmer continued for half an hour before the curd was allowed to settle. After this all the whey was removed.

The curd consolidated, forming a texture like that of firm foam-rubber. This was cut into manageable sections about five inches (127 mm) wide. During the next process, the 'cheddaring', these pieces were turned over and placed on top of one another a number of times while they drained and the amount of lactic acid in the curd increased. All this took about an hour. The lumps of curd were then broken up by hand and cooled for a while before 'vatting' into the moulds. After being pressed for an hour they were taken out again, broken up and fed through a mill. Salt was added to the freshly ground curd before it was finally packed into the moulds and pressed.

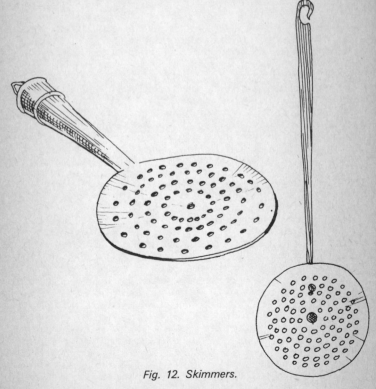

Fig. 12. Skimmers.

To make the cheeses more attractive to the customer, colouring may well have been added to the milk at an early stage. (Originally colour was added to a skim-milk cheese to give an appearance of full-milk richness.) In the sixteenth century saffron, long a food flavouring and yarn dye, was used in the West Country. The plant used was the true saffron (*Crocus sativus*) and not the similar but poisonous meadow saffron or autumn crocus *(Colchicum autumnale)*. The red styles of the saffron were taken from the flowers when they were harvested and dried on canvas in kilns by the growers, who were known as 'crockers'. The harvest yielded about 20 lb (9 kg) of saffron to the acre. Other colouring agents like carrot juice were used in some areas, and in the eighteenth century anatta or anatto was introduced. An extract from the fruit of a West Indian tree, *Bixa orelana,* it was cheaper than saffron and is still the most satisfactory way of colouring cheese.

This system of cheesemaking, as standardised by Harding, was soon used by many of the dairies in the West Country, Gloucestershire and Scotland and was adopted to some extent by the makers of Cheshire and other hard-pressed cheeses.

Cheddars were by now being made in cheeses of 80 lb (36 kg) rather than of 150 lb (68 kg) or even 200 lb (91 kg) and fewer dairies were storing cheeses for more than five to twelve months. This would have disappointed Archdeacon Denison, who preserved a piece of Cheddar under a glass on his hall table for forty-one years, maintaining that 'it may be hard, but it is still sweet'.

The great West Pennard Cheddar

Not far from Harding's birthplace lies the small village of West Pennard, a few miles to the east of Glastonbury and within sight of the famous Tor. Here, in the heart of the cheese and cider making country, one of England's greatest cheeses was made — great in size but unfortunately not in flavour. The loyal farmers of the village collected together the milk of 730 cows and made one vast cheese which they patriotically presented to Queen Victoria on the occasion of her wedding in 1841.

Weighing 11 cwt (559 kg) and measuring 9 feet 4 inches (2.845m) in circumference, this huge token of respect was graciously accepted by the monarch, but never eaten. For before she had time to taste it — which may have been just as well — the proud farmers of West Pennard requested its return on loan in order to exhibit it around the country. After being shown and no doubt prodded by the inquisitive during its tour, the somewhat battered cheese was not so welcome a second time on its return to the palace. The Queen refused to accept the now well-matured tribute from West Pennard and returned it to its makers, who

17

could not now decide its ownership in view of their varied contribution and argued over the aging cheese until it was no longer fit for human consumption. It was eventually fed to the local swine.

A few carved replicas of the wooden follower used to press the royal coat of arms into the ill-fated cheese when it was pressed survive. One of these replicas was presented to the village and now hangs in the village hall.

The farmers of West Pennard were chosen to make another royal cheese on behalf of the cheesemakers of the south-west of England. Not so large, but certainly more acceptable, their new gift was presented to Queen Elizabeth II on the occasion of her Silver Jubilee in 1977, after being shown at the two hundredth Bath and West Show, which was for the first time the Royal Bath

Fig. 13. A replica (1840) of the follower for the great West Pennard cheese made in 1839 for Queen Victoria.

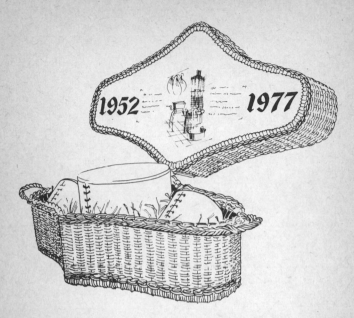

Fig. 14. The Jubilee cheeses made in West Pennard and presented to Queen Elizabeth II by the cheesemakers of south-west England in 1977.

and West Show. The present cheesemakers of West Pennard, H. G. Green and Sons, lavished their skill on three cheeses, two small truckles of 9 lb (4.08 kg) and one great cheese of almost 90 lb (40.8 kg). They were again made from the milk of several local farms, at least one of which had provided milk for Victoria's ill-fated gift. These new royal cheeses were made in the traditional farmhouse manner and pressed in an old cast-iron press made years before in Chard and still in daily use, before being dressed in the original way. The largest cheese was laced into a corset-like bandage of strong linen as it was too big for the thin cotton cheesecloths to support. The cheeses were stored from October 1976 to June 1977 before receiving their final preparation for the show and afterwards they were taken to the palace in a specially made basket.

Cheddar-making today

The basic process of making Cheddar has changed little since Harding's day, but the equipment has altered greatly, as have the

19

standards of hygiene. The chemical changes that take place during the process are now understood and so control over these changes can be better regulated during manufacture and storage.

The great improvement in winter quarters and winter feeding for the cattle, with good silage, has made it possible to make a high-quality cheese all the year round, instead of just during the summer months. The milk collected from the milking parlours is now pasteurised before the cheesemaking commences: the milk is heated to a temperature of 161F (72C) for a period of 12 to 18 seconds, killing the bacteria in it. Opponents of pasteurisation point out that all bacteria in the cheese are killed anyway during the first sixty days of maturing and that the pre-heating possibly affects the flavour. One important advantage of the present system is that it enables the milk from different herds to be mixed.

Because the bacteria are killed during pasteurisation one of the important natural processes has to be replaced, the essential part of it being the production of lactic acid as the milk sours. In unpasteurised milk this was produced overnight in the milk kept from the previous evening. These bacteria are now replaced by a laboratory-incubated culture referred to as the *starter*. Farms hold stocks of the starter, kept in a deep-freeze until needed; it is inoculated into a small quantity of milk the day before it is required. Under the right conditions this culture then develops in the milk, producing a yogurt-like mixture which is added to the milk during cheesemaking.

The starter is added to the freshly pasteurised milk at 85F (29 C) and is allowed to ripen for between 30 and 45 minutes. Colouring is often put in at this stage: anatto, in an alcoholic soda solution, is added with four to six times its own bulk of water. Rennet is also added now, while the milk is stirred continually.

Rennet. Rennet is the coagulating agent which encloses the fat globules and separates the milk into curds and whey. In the past coagulating agents such as the milk of fig trees, teasel flowers, butterwort and lady's bedstraw were used. Lady's bedstraw was known in the eighteenth century as the cheese-rennet herb. But these long ago gave way to rennet obtained from vells, the lining of the fourth, digestive stomach of a calf; they are dried, cleaned, then soaked in brine to extract the ferment. It is now produced in sterile and hygienic conditions very different from when the farmer's wife made her own: even though she may have filtered the extract through sand and charcoal, it often contained many impurities.

The high cost of commercial rennet makes it important to purchase only as much as is needed immediately. To check doubtful rennet, one drop in a teaspoon of milk should coagulate it in five minutes. Before being added to the milk the rennet should be diluted with four times its own bulk of water to assist dispersal through the milk; undiluted rennet would cause instant coagulation in the area to which it was added. After adding the rennet the stirring is continued for a further five to ten minutes to mix it well.

The modern cheesemaking vat is of stainless steel with a surrounding steel jacket which can be filled with steam to regulate the temperature. The contents are stirred with large stirrers which are also used as the cutting knives in the next stage, after the coagulation is complete.

The coagulated curd is ready to cut when the curd breaks cleanly above a finger inserted just below the surface at an angle or when the curd breaks easily from the edge of the vat when eased away. The cutting should reduce the curd to lumps about the size of a pea and at this time the level of acidity should be 0.14 to 0.17 per cent.

Acidity. The level of lactic-acid production during cheesemaking dictates the timetable of the whole process. Nowadays the acidity is usually tested by the Lloyd's acidity test, using sodium hydroxide and phenol phthalein as an indicator (see Chapter 6).

The next step is the scalding, which is done by means of the steam heating jacket. The temperature is raised to 104-106F (40-41C) over a period of nearly an hour. Care must be taken not to hurry this as it may slow down the acidity production. After scalding the acidity level should be 0.18 to 0.19 per cent.

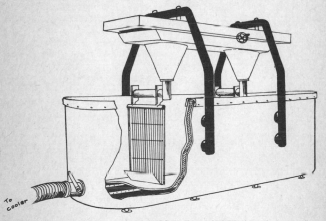

Fig. 15. Modern cheese vat of 2500 gallons (7365 litres), cut away to show the steam jacket and the rotary knives which travel up and down the vat. The curds and whey are drawn off together, when ready, into a cooler.

The curds are now well separated from the whey, which is soon drawn off. The curds may be left in the vat to work the next stage there or curds and whey are drawn off together into a separate cooler out of which the whey is drained; the curds consolidate into one or two large lumps. After consolidation the actual 'cheddaring' takes place when these lumps are cut into blocks about 7 inches (180 mm) wide and left to drain for a further ten minutes. During the next forty minutes or so the blocks are turned and placed on top of each other a number of times until they are four or five high. While this is happening the curd continues to drain and the acidity rises to the level required for milling. The modern

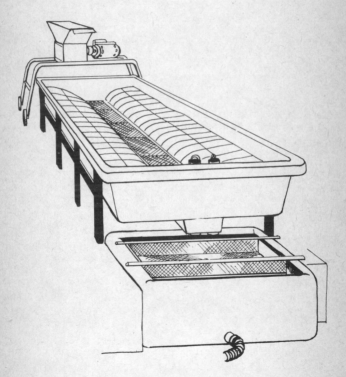

Fig. 16. Modern cooler containing settled curds cut and ready for cheddaring. The curd mill is at the far end. The whey drains off into the tank at the front, from where it is pumped to the separator.

Fig. 17. A Cheddar cheese store.

mill is a stainless-steel rotating cutter through which the curd blocks are fed; they are reduced to pieces about the size of potato chips. Salt is added at the same time in the proportion of 2lb to 100 gallons of milk (900g to 450 litres).

The resulting cut and salted curd is stirred by mechanical agitators or forked by hand to cool it before it is finally placed in the moulds.

After packing, the moulds which are lined with disposable cloths, are pre-pressed for a moment, either by machine or by leaving two or three moulds to stand on top of each other, to bind the curds together. Then they are placed in the modern hydraulic press. Fitting one into another, a dozen or more moulds may be placed in a press at a time. The greatest pressure is applied after one hour.

The next day the last stage, dressing the cheese, takes place. The cheese is removed from the press and scalded with hot water, which seals the surface, and is then returned to the press for a while. Later in the day the temporary cloths are removed, the cheese is sealed with grease and the traditional cotton cheesecloths are affixed. The grease, pure lard, may be applied direct to the cheese by hand or the cloths themselves may be immersed in molten lard and then hot water, wrung out, and then carefully wrapped around the cheese, which is returned to the press for a further twenty-four hours.

On its final removal from the moulds the cheese is marked with its date of manufacture, vat number and the farm of origin before being put into store. Each farm stores its own cheese for some time in conditions of controlled humidity and temperature, requiring the use of large dehumidifiers to extract excess moisture from the air. The cheese still requires careful attention: regular turning and cleaning is a continual task.

This basic method of making Cheddar has now been adopted by all the farms producing it, and indeed the factory process follows the same stages on a much larger scale — using tens of thousands of gallons of milk a day. Machine-wrapping with polythene has taken the place of the cheesecloth and production-flow timetables may have to be kept to, rather than the discerning standards of an experienced farmhouse cheesemaker.

3. Farmhouse or factory?

Throughout this book the term 'farmhouse cheese' refers to cheese that is still made on the farm in the traditional manner. The Milk Marketing Board restricts its use of the term 'Farmhouse Cheese', for marketing purposes, to certain Cheddar, Cheshire and Lancashire cheeses. These cheeses must be made on the farm but may contain a proportion of milk from neighbouring farms and are at present identified by the use of a trademark depicting three cheeses surrounded by the words 'Farmhouse English Cheese'.

The board's association with the farmhouse makers began in 1934 when they introduced a scheme to assist the makers through a period when the seasonal price fluctuations threatened to end production on a number of farms. By taking over the marketing of cheese and guaranteeing a price they managed to save a number of firms, but unfortunately the war put paid to many of these as milk was needed for the liquid market.

In 1954, at the request of the National Cheese Council, the board introduced the present Farmhouse Cheesemaking scheme, under which strict quality control is enforced. The cheese is graded and marketed through the board's own agents, the largest of whom is Crump Way Ltd of Wells, Somerset. They are responsible for collecting Cheddar from the farms of the south-west and their cheese store is the biggest in Europe. Emberton Brothers of Crewe collect and distribute for their area. This scheme has done a lot to save many of the smaller firms and ensure the continued manufacture of high-quality Farmhouse Cheese in the traditional manner.

4. Regional cheeses

Caerphilly

One of the problems of making Cheddar was the shortage of cash while the farmer was waiting at least five months for the cheese to mature. This was one of the reasons why at the end of the nineteenth century many of the West Country cheesemakers also began to make Caerphilly, which is ready to sell and eat within a few weeks of manufacture; making and selling this cheese saved a lot of small enterprises from closure.

Caerphilly is a semi-hard cheese which originated probably no earlier than 1800 in the Mid Glamorgan town from which it takes its name. It was always very popular with the miners of South Wales, being ideal for an underground lunch-box — its height of 2½ inches (64mm) is said to have made it easy to eat by hand down the mine without adding too much coal-dust.

Scalded at a slightly different temperature, Caerphilly is then cut by hand after the whey has been rapidly drained; it is salted and packed into the moulds, about 9 inches (230mm) in diameter. The whole process of making Caerphilly is worked at slightly lower acidity levels than Cheddar and, after pressing for one day, the cheese is removed and soaked in brine for a further twenty-four hours.

Ready to eat after only two weeks, Caerphilly has a close texture, white colour and a clean mild taste that goes down well with a glass of dry wine.

Cheshire

The oldest English cheese as it is known today, Cheshire was referred to in the Domesday Book; it was very popular at the Elizabethan court and gave its name to one of London's most famous pubs, Ye Old Cheshire Cheese in Fleet Street.

A hard-pressed cheese, now made under the Milk Marketing Board's control at twenty farms in the fertile plains of Cheshire and Salop, Cheshire cheese can be obtained in three colours, red, white and blue. The white and red are both soft crumbly cheeses weighing 10 to 50lb (4.5 to 22.7 kg), mild and mellow of flavour. Blue Cheshire is a much rarer cheese. It is made on only one farm, which produces about two hundred cheeses a week. Much appreciated by the connoisseur, these rich and creamy blue-veined cheeses deserve a fine vintage to accompany them on the table.

In the past the making of Cheshire was a quicker initial process than that of Cheddar. The whey was extracted as fast as possible and the curds were drained more thoroughly before being milled twice; this broke them up very finely before vatting. The vatted moulds were then kept overnight in a cheese oven at 90 to 100F (32-38C) and later stored in a warmer store than Cheddar was to ensure the short, open texture for which Cheshire is famous.

Derby

Another of the rarer cheeses, Derby is a quick ripening, hard-pressed cheese. Moister than Cheddar, though of a similar type, it is white and of close firm texture with a clean mild taste, best eaten six weeks after manufacture. Derby is made from the evening and morning milk with a full cream content, the finished cheeses being salted by hand all over until they have absorbed as much salt as is possible.

Sage Derby

This cheese has been known since about three hundred years ago, when Derby was mixed with both the leaves of sage and a tea made from them. The eating of Sage Derby was part of the traditional Christmas festivities; the sage was thought to be beneficial to health and to aid digestion of the cheese as well as improve its flavour. Sage was certainly regarded as a cure for impotence but it is doubtful if any great claims can be made for the medicinal properties of the commercial variety of Sage Derby that is available today.

Dunlop

Said originally to have been brought from Ireland to Scotland in the time of Charles II by Barbara Gilmore, Dunlop is often described as a Scottish Cheddar as there is no other comparable cheese. Dunlop should be uncoloured, smooth and moister than Cheddar. It is named after the village of Dunlop in Ayrshire.

Gloucester

This was once available as both Single and Double Gloucester according to size; the now popular Double Gloucester is another hard-pressed, moist cheese similar to Cheddar. It is milled slightly differently and is made in flat rounds of 9 to 30lb (4.08 to 13.61 kg). Now of a pale straw colour, close texture and mellow flavour, it was in the past painted red and must have made a fine sight being transported by barge to market in London.

The cheesemaking season for Gloucester used to open with a festival on 1st May in Randwick where three cheeses were decorated with flowers and carried through the village on a garlanded litter to the church. There they were taken off and rolled ceremonially round the churchyard three times before being replaced on the litter and taken back to the village green to be cut up and distributed to the inhabitants.

Another festivity connected with Gloucester is the Cheese

Rolling that takes place on Coopers Hill near the village of Brockworth. Formerly a Whit Monday custom, it has now been transferred to the Spring Bank Holiday. The youth of the village chase a cheese, encased in wood and decorated with ribbons, down the steep hill. The starter sends the cheese on its way at the count of three and the competitors follow at the count of four. The custom is said to have originated from the necessity annually to ensure the continuation of grazing rights on the common. Such importance was attached to the ceremony that even during the wartime days of food rationing races were still run after a wooden dummy, with only a small token of cheese for the winner. The Master of Ceremonies took the matter so seriously that one William Brookes, Master for fifty years, was even buried in his regalia — a white smock and a tall grey hat with ribbons on it.

Lancashire

Lancashire is the third cheese administered by the Milk Marketing Board Farmhouse Cheese Scheme and is made by only five farms at present, the rest coming from creameries.

Made in cheeses of 9 to 40lb (4.08 to 18.14 kg) it is a white hard-pressed cheese of buttery and open texture with a clean mild flavour. It is the softest of the hard-pressed cheeses and is probably what Ben Gunn dreamt of on *Treasure Island* when he sighed for toasted cheese, for Lancashire is possibly at its best when toasted.

It is still made as it was from the curds of two days' making and therefore only small quantities can be produced by the five farms, so the farmhouse product is hard to find, but well worth the search.

Leicester

Leicestershire cheeses, looking like orange millstones, are the most colourful of England's cheeses. A hard-pressed cheese with a granular texture, its clean fresh taste makes it an ideal dessert. Having a higher moisture content than Cheddar, Leicester is best eaten within ten to twelve weeks and will not improve with prolonged storage.

Stilton

One of the most famous cheeses in the world, Stilton has long been praised in prose and verse, by Pope, Jane Austen, Charles Lamb and many others. An open-textured white cheese, with the well-known blue veins, Stilton and fine port make the perfect end to a good meal.

Stilton's sudden rise to fame in the eighteenth century has been attributed to a number of people but it certainly owes much to a Mrs Paulet of Wymondham who made cheeses for a relative, the landlord of the Bell Inn, a coaching stop on the Great North Road at Stilton in Cambridgeshire. Sold there from the 1730s by the host, Cooper Thornhill, it rapidly achieved fame and sold for the then amazing price of two shillings and sixpence a pound by 1745. Mrs Paulet's recipe was still being used in the twentieth century.

However, ten years before Mrs Paulet's cheese arrived, in 1724, Defoe wrote of Stilton when on his tour that it was 'brought to the table with mites or maggots round so thick that they bring a spoon with them for you to eat the mites with as you do the cheese'. Today Stilton can only be made in the Vale of Belvoir, the valley of the Dove and parts of Nottinghamshire.

Approximately 16 gallons (73l) of milk are required to make a traditional Stilton of 13 or 14lb (5.90 to 6.35 kg). After making the curd, it is carefully broken up by hand, instead of milling, into pieces the size of walnuts and hazelnuts before being packed by hand into the moulds or hoops. Each mould is placed on a board covered with a straw cheese mat or calico cloth. The smaller pieces of curd are put in first and last, surrounding the largest pieces in the middle, until a total of about 30lb (13.6 kg) is packed into the mould. As the whey drains from the curd the top hoops or steel rings may be taken off. Turned initially twice in two hours and again after eight hours, the Stilton should not require pressing. It is then turned daily for a week before it is ready to leave the mould.

Out of the mould, Stilton has a greasy appearance and still requires a lot of work. It has to be scraped all over with a knife to fill the cracks and give it a smooth surface before it is bandaged with a cheesecloth. The mould is then replaced to support the cheese and the whole process is repeated on the following two days before the cheese is put in the drying room at a temperature of 60F (16C). Here the bandage is renewed on the two following days. After ten days the distinctive, crinkly coat begins to form. The atmosphere during this time must be kept sufficiently moist to prevent cracking and hardness.

Two weeks later the cheese will be ready for the ripening room or cellar, where the air must be humid. After four months of daily turning the fine Stilton flavour and famous blue mould develop; during this time the cheese loses about 55 per cent of its weight from the time of curding.

A good Stilton should have a uniform brown crinkly surface and yield on pressure from the thumb; its cut surface should show the blue veins distinct from the curd, which should be white in appearance and not yellow. It should have a rich mellow flavour; the mould should not predominate, nor should there be an acid or pungent taste, and the texture should be moist and creamy.

During its time in the store Stilton is often subject to the dreaded cheese mite. Though quite harmless and once considered essential by many, mite can nowadays be prevented by chemical spraying in the stores as well as by careful brushing, scrubbing and scalding of the cheese.

Such is the work required to make a Stilton that a certain Mrs Musson of Warnaby, a noted dairy woman in her day, remarked to Rider Haggard that 'except that they make no noise, Stiltons are more trouble than babies'.

Wensleydale

Another semi-hard cheese, Yorkshire Wensleydale is a white cheese of mild flavour and was once the exclusive recipe of the Cistercian monks of Jervaulx Abbey, who had brought it with them from the Continent as a ewes' milk cheese. After the dissolution, the coveted recipe is said to have fallen into the hands of the landlord of the Cover Bridge Inn nearby, where it became known as Cover Bridge cheese for some time before changing its name to Wensleydale.

Wensleydale is made in a similar way to Derbyshire. The evening's milk was renneted on leaving the 'baulks' (a Yorkshire name for a small stone-built cow byre). The curd was cut and drained in a muslin bag and added to the next morning's milk after that, too, had been turned into curd and drained. The Wensleydale method required only a slight pressure on the moulds, which held 10 to 12lb (4.54 to 5.44 kg) of cheese each. There is also a Blue Wensleydale which is considered by many to be even better than Stilton when kept for four or five months.

A few unusual Scottish cheeses

Ayrshire is a soft creamy cheese of nutty flavour. *Caboc*, a soft almost white cheese, is made in the Highlands from double cream and covered in toasted pinhead oatmeal. *Hramsa*, which means 'all healing', is a soft cheese made from double cream and flavoured with wild garlic; it is made in the Highlands. *Morven* is a mild cheese of full flavour made in squares and sometimes flavoured with caraway.

5. Lost and disappearing cheeses

Bath cheese

Last seen at the beginning of the twentieth century, Bath cheese was a soft cream cheese made in 9-inch (230 mm) squares 1 inch (25 mm) deep and had a rather fresh, acid flavour.

Cambridge

Another soft cheese sold when only a few days old, Cambridge cheese is possibly still available in the Ely area.

Colwick

A soft cheese very similar to Cambridge, Colwick was made up to and just after the Second World War.

Cotherstone

A double cream cheese, white or blue-veined and similar to Wensleydale, Cotherstone was made in Swaledale and sometimes called Yorkshire Stilton.

Dorset Blue or Blue Vinny

A very scarce blue-veined cheese, Dorset Blue is made, it appears, by one person in the Cerne Abbas area near Dorchester. At one time it was spoken of as being so hard 'that softer missiles have been fired from cannon'. Blue Vinny was a hard-pressed cheese of crumbly texture with distinctive blue veins which gave it its name, *vinny* being an old local word for mould.

It seems that more Dorset Blue is sold than is made! The English Country Cheese Council say that: 'It is very unlikely that you will find any farm today making Blue Vinny cheese although a number of retailers offer it for sale. In our experience we find on investigation it is an over-matured Stilton type, quite unlike the genuine Dorset cheese.' As the original Blue Vinny was made from skimmed milk, one would be unable to sell it under the present marketing arrangements, which insist on full-cream milk being used.

The recipe of Blue Vinny has long been a closely guarded secret. It is known that blue veining could be introduced by taking in curds from the previous day's making and in other ways — rather than by the farmer washing his harness in the whey, as legend has it. At Swanage in Dorset before the Second World War Blue Vinny cheeses were left standing under the beer-barrel taps in the Black Swan inn.

Newmarket

Another lost cheese, small and rich, Newmarket was kept to mature well before eating. *The Complete Housewife or Accomplished Gentlewoman's Companion* gave the recipe in 1729:

To Make a Newmarket Cheese to Eat at Two Years Old

Any morning in September take twenty quarts of new milk warm from the cow, and colour it with Marigolds (an orange pigment being pressed from the petals of the pot marigold, *Calendula officinalis*). When this is done, and the milk not cold, get ready a quart of cream and a quart of fair water, which must be kept stirring over the fire till it is scalding hot, then stir well into the milk and rennet, as you do other cheese; when it is come, lay

30

cheesecloths over it, and settle it with your hands, the more hands the better; as the whey rises take it away, and when it is clean gone, put your curd into your fat (mould), breaking it as little as you can, then put it in the press, and press it gently an hour, take it out again, and cut it then in thin slices, and lay them singly on a cloth, and wipe them dry; then put it in a tub, and break it with your hands as small as you can, and mix it with a good handful of salt and a quart of cold cream; put it in the fat and lay a pound weight on it till next day; then press and order it as others.

York

This was a soft cheese like Cambridge and Colwick.

6. Making your own cheese

A small Cheddar

It is quite easy to make a small, hard-pressed cheese of the Cheddar type without too much expensive equipment and without the use of a starter.

Equipment
Pail
Large pan sufficient to take 3 gallons (13.6l)
Ladle or skimmer
Carving knife
Mould to take 3lb (1.36 kg) cheese
Dairy thermometer
Cheesecloth
Press (both this and the mould can be home-made; see pages 34-5)

The evening's milk should be warmed indirectly, by placing it in a container in a pail of hot water, until the temperature is raised to 90F (32C). Then strain the milk through a cloth into a warm pan, cover, and keep in a warm place until morning. During this time the bacteria in the milk are starting to increase the level of lactic acid.

Heat the morning's milk similarly and add to the evening's milk, so that the temperature of the whole quantity is raised to 85F (29C).

Renneting. Stir in a teaspoonful of rennet mixed with four teaspoonfuls of water (one teaspoon of rennet for every 3 gallons, 13.6l of milk) and leave for forty-five minutes to one hour.

When the milk is set into a junket-like consistency that breaks cleanly over a finger inserted at an angle, cut the curd with the carving knife, across both ways and then again with the knife at an angle, so that the curd is cut into small diamond-shaped pieces. Using the skimmer or ladle, cut the curd further by passing the skimmer back and forth, working from just below the surface to the bottom of the pan. When the curd is cut into pieces the size of peas cover the pan with a cheesecloth and leave for about five minutes.

Scalding. The following process sounds complicated but is really quite easy and one soon gets used to it.

The temperature of the curds and whey has to be raised to 95F (35C). This is done by removing about one fifth of the milk, heating it indirectly as before and returning it to the pan. The increase in temperature of the extracted portion necessary to raise the temperature of the main pan to 95F (35C) can be calculated. The total number of gallons or litres of milk is multiplied by the number of degrees it needs to be raised and then divided by the number of gallons (litres) heated.

$$\frac{\text{total gallons (litres) x degrees required to be raised}}{\text{number of gallons (litres) heated}} \quad = \quad \begin{array}{l}\text{necessary temperature}\\\text{rise of the heated}\\\text{milk}\end{array}$$

e.g. 20 gallons of milk at 80F are to be raised to 84F. 4 gallons extracted, therefore the temperature rise of that 4 gallons must be:

$$\frac{20 \times 4}{4} \quad = \quad 20F$$

As milk should not be heated to very high temperatures when cheesemaking, i.e. no more than 100F (37C), it is best to repeat the heating and returning process a number of times. The milk is stirred continually, especially when adding warm milk, until a temperature of 95F (35C) is reached in about half an hour. This system can be used for all cheesemaking where no heated vat is available.

Continue to stir until the curd is firm but not hard. Then allow the curd to settle for about fifteen minutes before pouring off as much whey as possible, straining it through a cheesecloth.

The cheesecloth, with any crumbs of curd, is then placed over a bath and the curd from the pan is tipped into it. Take care to break the curd as little as possible. Take the corners of the cloth and tie it into a tight bundle, then turn it over on to its knot and leave for forty minutes.

Open the bundle and cut up the curd into 2 inch (50mm) cubes, tie up again and leave for a further twenty minutes. Open the bundle a second time and pull the cubes apart before retying. Repeat this process a number of times at longer intervals of thirty to forty-five minutes.

When a distinct acid smell can be detected the hot iron test should be made (see page 37). The threads should draw to ¾ inch (19mm). Break the curd up with the hands into pieces the size of cherries, add salt at the ratio of 1 oz (28.35g) to every 2 gallons (9.1

litres) of milk and mix thoroughly. The curd is now ready to put into the mould and press.

First line the mould with coarse cloth, such as hessian, fill with curds and then place the followers above the cheese and press. The followers must be deep enough to remain clear of the mould when it is under pressure. The next morning remove the cheese from the mould, bathe it with hot water and replace in the mould in a cotton cloth. An hour or so later take the cheese from the mould again, grease with lard and dress with the cloth bandage, then replace in the press for a further day.

Greasing. Either lard can be smeared directly on to the cheese cold, or — much easier if a number of cheeses are to be done — the actual cheesecloth can be immersed in molten lard and wrung out, then immersed briefly in hot water and wrung out before being wrapped around the cheese. Ensure that there is a good

Fig. 18. Home-made moulds fashioned from tin cans.

overlap so that the cheese does not break out at the join later. Cloth caps, smaller pieces of cheesecloth treated in the same way, are placed top and bottom first, the turnover from these being covered by the larger cloth.

Moulds. Moulds of various shapes and sizes made from stainless steel, tinned metal and polythene can be purchased from a number of firms, but a small cheese mould is not difficult to make at very little cost. Good stout food tins of the right size can be used, keeping the lid to use as a pattern for the follower. Another ideal material is a plastic drainpipe cut to the length required. All moulds will require a few small holes to be drilled around the sides to allow the whey to drain.

Presses. There are at least two kinds of press on the market and one of them has the added advantage of doubling as a wine press. The manufactured presses are certainly easy to use and take up less room than some of the strange devices used by many home

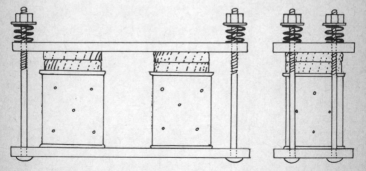

Fig. 19. Home-made presses.

cheesemakers, although most of these have done their job successfully.

One of the easiest home-made presses is based on a medieval design and is very cheap and efficient provided one has the space. It is easily made by fixing one end of a metal bar or wooden beam under a ledge, or a groove cut in a tree is sufficient. A short distance from the fixed end a vertical bar is attached which transmits the weight to the cheese. The weights are then placed along the bar at the distance that gives the required pressure. For instance a 56lb (25.40 kg) weight on a bar about 10 feet (3m) long exerts a pressure of about 500lb (226.80 kg) which is sufficient for a small cheese over a period of a few days, although the greater the pressure the firmer the cheese and up to 2 tons (2.03 t) can be used on larger cheeses.

Another simple press that works reasonably well can be made from two stout planks and four long bolts, washers and four strong coil springs. Set up the planks as illustrated in fig. 19. This arrangement makes an effective press when the nuts are tightened up at the beginning and again about an hour later as the cheese compresses. Without the springs continual tightening is required to maintain a constant pressure.

Errors that might occur include overstirring and excess renneting. A curd that has been overstirred, i.e. cut smaller than usual by mistake, during renneting should be cut rather larger than usual, stirred less and scalded at a slightly lower temperature. If too much rennet has been added by mistake, cut and heat earlier, scald lower and try to retain moisture so that the curd is not too hard and dry when milled.

Acidity levels and testing

Throughout the cheesemaking process a continual watch is kept on the rising level of the lactic acid which dictates the pace of the operations. This is done by chemical testing.

Equipment

An acidimeter consisting of:

1.5 cubic inch (25 cc) graduated burette with tap and stand

0.6 cubic inch (10 cc) pipette

A small mixing dish

A dropper bottle of phenol phthalein

Sodium hydroxide solution (sometimes referred to as No. 9)

Method. Fill the burette with sodium hydroxide to the level 0 on the scale.

Collect 0.6 cubic inches (10 cc) of the whey or milk to be tested in the pipette and release it into the mixing bowl placed beneath the burette.

Add three drops of the phenol phthalein to the whey.

Then very slowly add the solution from the burette above, stirring continually. As soon as any pinkish colour appears proceed with caution, stirring all the time. As it is stirred the colour appears and disappears while the solution is added. The moment the colour remains permanent stop.

The acidity is then read from the scale on the burette thus: 0.1 cubic inches (1.7 cc) equals 0.17 per cent acidity.

The advantage of this testing is that it can be used as an in-

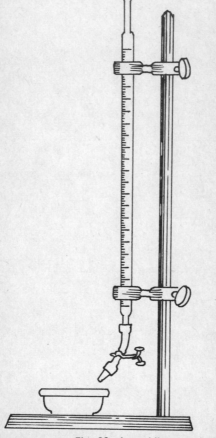

Fig. 20. An acidimeter.

dicator during the whole cheesemaking process. Tests taken before renneting, after scalding, before drawing off the whey and from the curd as it drains during cheddaring give an indication of the speed of the progress and whether it is a 'fast' or 'slow' cheese.

Hot iron test. This test is rather frowned upon by some of the more scientific cheesemakers but it is very simple and has long been used with good results. The only equipment needed is a small piece of cleaned iron, say 1 inch (25 mm) wide by ¼ inch (6 mm) thick, fitted to a wooden handle if desired.

Heat the iron to black heat (red hot and then cooled). Take a small piece of squeezed dry curd and rub it on the iron, draw the curd away carefully and the length of the thread attached to the iron shows the state of the cheese: ¼ inch (6 mm) threads — 0.18 to 0.19 acidity; 1½ to 1¾ inch (38 to 45 mm) threads — 0.8 to 0.9 acidity.

The correct acidity of the curd at milling is most important and this varies from dairy to dairy according to the natural acidity of the milk, which depends on the pastures used for grazing and the type of ground beneath. Cheddar is milled at 0.85 per cent in some dairies but equally good results may be obtained at 0.56 per cent elsewhere.

The level of acidity during the process can be controlled in a number of ways, which are generally related to the amount of moisture retained at the various stages. Firstly, a weak starter can cause a slow cheese, as can scalding too high or too fast. The use of milk from cows that have been recently treated with penicillin will also cause a breakdown in acidity growth.

If the starter is found to have been weak and the acidity is too low, the curd should be cut larger and scalded at a slightly lower temperature.

If the acidity after scalding is low, delay draining the whey from the curd for some time; the retained heat will assist acid growth.

If low readings continue after draining, pile the curd higher during cheddaring and cover with cloths to prevent a hardening of the outer surface of the curds.

Making a large Cheddar

This recipe is for making Cheddar in larger quantities, with the use of a starter and special equipment such as a vat, cheese knives and an acidimeter.

Pour the evening milk into the vat through a filter: a metal sieve used in conjunction with some sort of material such as flannelette should remove most impurities. If the weather is warm cool the milk to 65F (18C). The following morning skim off the cream and add the starter to the milk in a proportion of ¼ to 2 per cent, depending on the acidity of the milk. If there is only 0.18 per cent acidity add 2 per cent starter, less if the acidity is higher. Heat the removed cream indirectly to 90F (32C) and pour back through the strainer. Add the morning's milk and raise the temperature of the whole to 84F (29C).

When the milk is the correct temperature and the acidity reaches 0.21 to 0.22 per cent add the rennet at the rate of 4oz per 100 gallons of milk (100g to 400l), the rennet first being mixed with four times its own bulk of water. The rennet must be stirred well into the milk to prevent instant, lumpy coagulation.

The curd will now start to set into a junket-like mass and should be ready to cut in 45 to 60 minutes; test as for the small Cheddar. Cut it both ways and again if necessary until the curd is cut into pieces the size of peas. Remove any curd that may have stuck to the sides and bottom if possible.

The next step, the scalding, should be done very gradually (one degree Fahrenheit every three minutes), raising the temperature to 104F (40C) over an hour, whilst stirring gently all the time.

When the scald is over, the acidity, which will have dropped after renneting, should have risen by 0.03 per cent to 0.19 or 0.20 per cent and the curd should then be allowed to settle if the draining and cheddaring is to be done in the vat. Alternatively drain off the curds and whey together into a separate cooler when available, and the whey may be drained off separately from this.

The curd should then consolidate into a lump ready for ripening and cheddaring. This is done by cutting the curd into pieces about 9 inches by 4 inches (230mm by 100mm), which are then turned and placed on top of each other. Repeat this turning after ten minutes, piling the curd three pieces high, and again after fifteen minutes to four pieces high, and fifteen minutes later again to five pieces high. During the cheddaring, test the acidity from time to time from the drainings and when it reaches the required level it is ready to mill and salt.

The curd must be cut into pieces the size of potato chips and salt added at the rate of 2lb (0.9 kg) per 100 gallons (454.6l) of milk. Mix the salt well in and fork the curd about until it is no more than 70F (21C); then it is ready for vatting (pressing).

Press the curd firmly into the moulds, which are lined with a coarse cloth or the plastic disposable cloths that are now available. Pre-press for a few minutes — standing one mould on top of another three or four high should be sufficient to do this. The moulds are now ready to put into the press. The old upright cast-iron weight and lever press will take two large moulds one above the other of four truckles in pairs side by side if the followers are carefully levelled up.

The pressure must be applied lightly at first before being increased to its maximum an hour later. The treatment following this is the same as that for the small Cheddar — scalding, greasing and dressing.

Caerphilly

Caerphilly is a very easy and practical cheese to make in reasonable quantities; it does not require the use of a mill and can be eaten within a short time.

Process the evening and morning milk as for Cheddar but heat the whole to 86F (30C) and add rennet at 0.18 per cent acidity. When ready, cut into pieces a little larger than the Cheddar. Leave for ten minutes, then stir gently for thirty minutes, during which time the curd is scalded to 88F (31C). When the scalding is complete and the acidity is 0.16 per cent draw off the whey and allow the curd to drain. After half an hour cut the curd into 3-inch (75mm) cubes, pile the curd up at the sides of the vat or cooler and allow it to drain for a further thirty minutes. Now break the curd up into small pieces, cutting both lengthways and across with a large single-bladed knife, then again with the knife held at an angle. Add 1oz (28.35g) of salt for every 3lb (1.36 kg) of curd and mix the curd thoroughly before vatting. Plastic moulds are available for the 9lb (4.08 kg) Caerphilly. Line these with cloth, fill and leave standing on top of one other for an hour before placing in the press. Remove them after two or three hours, take each cheese out of its cloth and turn it over, making sure to pull the cloth well up at the sides before returning it to the press overnight. The next day remove the cheeses and immerse them in a strong brine bath for two days. The cheeses will be ready to eat in a few weeks.

Cottage cheese

Hardly more than flavoured curds, cottage cheese is very easily made with little equipment.

Separate the milk into curds and whey using either rennet or lemon juice (half a lemon to 1 pint (0.57l) of milk). Place a piece of muslin that has been scalded in boiling water in a strainer and pour the curds into it. Bring the ends together and tie into a bag, which is then left to drain over a basin for twenty-four hours. Open the bag then, break up the curds with a fork and add salt and pepper as desired. Chopped chives make a pleasant addition.

Cream cheese

Here is an eighteenth-century recipe 'to make a summer cream-cheese':

Take 3 pints (1.70l) of milk just from the cow, and 5 pints (2.84l) of good sweet cream, which you must boil free from smoke; then put it to your milk, cool it till it is but blood-warm, and then put in a spoonful of rennet: when it is well come, take a large strainer, lay it in a great cheese-fat, then put the curd in gently upon the strainer, and when all the curd is in, lay on the cheese board, and a weight of 2lb (0.9 kg); let it so drain three hours, till the whey be well drained from it: then lay a cheesecloth in your lesser cheese-fat, and put in the curd, laying the cloth smooth over it as before, the board on top of that, and a 4lb (1.81 kg) weight on it; turn it every two hours into dry cloths before night, and be careful not to break it next morning; salt it, and keep it in the fat till next day; then put it into a wet cloth, which you must shift every day till it is ripe.

Record-keeping

If one is considering making cheese regularly it is advisable to keep a record of the process on each occasion. Well-kept records can be a great help in tracing mistakes or finding how the best cheese was made — it may be tasted months later. In order to check the progress of each cheese, each one should be marked with its date or a number in order to trace it in the records. A suggested record book for Cheddar might contain the following columns:

Date (or cheese number)
Gallons (litres) of milk
Quantity of starter
Time when starter was added
Acidity at renneting
Quantity of rennet
Time when rennet was added
Cutting time
Time at start of scald
Time at end of scald
Acidity at end of scald
Acidity before draining whey
Time of draining whey
Acidity at milling
Time of milling
Amount of salt
Remarks (i.e. soft curd, dry curd, slow cheese, etc)
A note of which starter was used if a number of strains are available

Showing and judging cheese

A great deal of experience and satisfaction can be had from showing cheese anywhere from the local flower and produce show to the large agricultural show.

Select your best cheese, but not one that has been bored with a tester (or 'cheese iron'). The judges' first impressions are important so make sure that the cheese chosen has a good shape with clean edges and a flat top and bottom — the result of regular turning in the store. After the cloths have been removed, the cheese can be washed and scrubbed or carefully scraped over with a knife to give the outer surface a facelift. It can then be polished with a grease or oil that does not affect the flavour or odour. A good clean linen bandage round the cheese also looks very tidy and efficient.

The judging of cheeses, whether for show or not, is an interesting test of one's work; the system used to grade Farmhouse Cheese by the Milk Marketing Board gives some idea of what to look for. The grader gives marks out of a hundred in the following manner:

Flavour and aroma	maximum 40 points
Body and texture	maximum 40 points
Finish	maximum 15 points
Colour	maximum 5 points
Total	100 points

For Cheddar the ideal characteristics are:

Flavour — mild and full, not strong, acid or biting; nutty aroma free from any taints.

Body and texture — smooth and close, no openness or visible moisture, not crumbly, and free from stickiness. On the cheese iron it should come out nearly solid and smooth; it should break off the iron easily, not bend, and show a flaky break.

Finish — trim and upstanding, free from cracks and mould defects.

Colour — pale and uniform, colouring should be even and not mottled.

A 'blown' cheese is produced when the cheese inflates, giving a rounded surface at the top or bottom, caused by gases forming within the cheese; it should not be considered for showing. The gas can be released, however, by piercing the cheese from the side just under the blown top or bottom and turning it over blown side down. Stand clear for a few moments or else you will inhale a most noxious odour.

Whey butter

When you are making cheese in any quantity the whey drained off should never be wasted. It can be used for animal food or, better still, cream and possibly butter.

In a modern dairy a large separator is used to extract the cream from the whey. It spins at thousands of revolutions a minute and the centrifugal force separates the solids from the liquids in the whey as it passes through a number of conical plates. Small hand separators can sometimes be found in farm sales and they will do the job; alternatively the whey can be collected in a flat container which will not taint it and left overnight for the cream to rise. Next morning carefully skim the cream from the surface. The cream should then be placed in a vessel and heated in water to 150F

(66C). It can then be used to pour or kept in a refrigerator until there is sufficient for buttermaking.

A number of small commercial butter churns are available for the home dairy from smallholding and self-sufficiency suppliers. Water is added to the cream, so that it is not too solid and is ready for buttermaking. Churn steadily until the butter 'comes', a task that may be over in twenty minutes or may last an hour or more. With the closed wooden type of churn, stop when the little glass peephole clears of liquid and check progress.

If a witch should happen to pop her head in the dairy while you are buttermaking and if you should happen to turn her away empty-handed, then beware, for it is unlikely that your butter will

Fig. 21. A wooden butter churn.

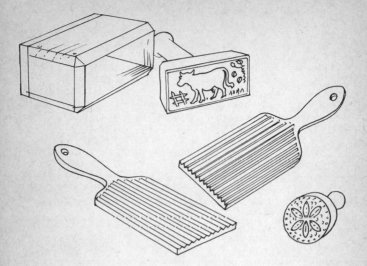

Fig. 22. Butter prints and Scotch hands.

ever come, unless you tie an old boot to the churn, an age-old remedy for such a misfortune.

A slow-coming butter might also respond to the following rhyme if it is repeated three times:

> Come, butter, come,
> Come, butter, come,
> Peter stands at the gate
> Waiting for a buttered cake,
> Come, butter, come.

When it has come and is in a granule-like state the butter should be washed, and salted if desired, then patted and shaped with a pair of wooden butter hands or 'Scotch hands'; one can serve curled butter at the table, or with a little searching carved wooden butter prints can be found to make decorated butter pats.

It should be remembered though that the fat gained for whey cream is more valuable in the cheese than in butter, so a larger than usual amount of cream may mean a bonus in butter, but at the loss of precious cheese.

Any whey left from the cream-making can still be used as a high-quality pig food: there is no need to waste anything in the process of cheesemaking.

7. Buying, keeping and serving cheese

Buying cheese

'When you buy cheese observe the coat, for if the cheese be old, and its coat be rough, rugged, or dry at the top, it indicates mites, or little worms. If it be spungy, moist, or full of holes it is subject to maggots. If you perceive on the outside any perished place, be sure to examine its deepness.' So wrote Mrs E. Smith in her *Complete Housewife* of 1729.

Fortunately mites and maggots are no longer a hazard, though care should still be taken in buying cheese. Advice is available to shops from the Milk Marketing Board's different departments, but still there are those that do not take care of their cheese as they should.

Any good store or delicatessen that is proud of its cheese selection should always let you sample a small piece before buying. Their attitude to such a request will show how interested they are in their customers and their stock. Buy your cheese from a shop that is busy enough to turn over its stock regularly and does not have cut, open cheese standing around day after day. Remember that only cheese labelled 'Farmhouse English Cheese' must have been made in a farm dairy; other cheeses need not have been made in the same rural way. In general, though, factory creameries are situated in the traditional cheesemaking areas, surrounded by the pastures that have provided the milk for cheese for centuries, and the system, though vast and mechanical, is based on the traditional processes and basic recipes.

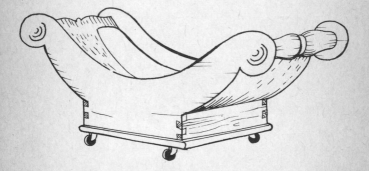

Fig. 23. A wooden cheese coaster, c. 1760.

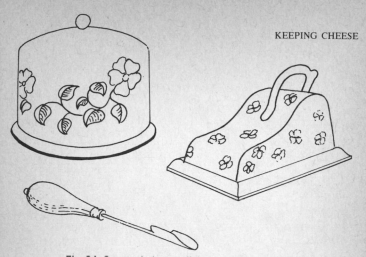

Fig. 24. Covered cheese dishes and a Stilton scoop.

Keeping cheese

Store the cheese in a refrigerator, but make sure that it is very well wrapped in polythene or foil to prevent drying out, and always remove it to room temperature for at least half an hour before it is needed. Do not change the temperature of the cheese too often. If you have a large cheese, it is best to cut what you need for the next few days rather than continually to take the whole cheese in and out of the refrigerator. However, most authorities argue against the use of a refrigerator at all and recommend covering it with a piece of muslin wrung out in a salt solution, which keeps the cheese moist and fresh.

Serving cheese past and present

In the mid eighteenth century fine wooden coasters with elegantly turned handles at each end were made. They held both a cheese and some bread and could be pushed along the table on little castors. Later, the Victorians had decorative pottery cheese dishes and covers, which can still be found today. In the age of Victorian table gadgetry a silver cheese scoop for Stilton was invented; it had a lever that could be depressed to eject the cheese on to the plate. Scooping Stilton from the middle of the cheese is a custom that survives; though quaint and old-fashioned, it can waste a large amount of excellent cheese, as this method causes the centre to crumble and dry out.

Cheese looks its best when at its most natural, served on a wooden cheeseboard, leaving ample room between the pieces. There should be a knife to cut each different variety when strong and mild cheeses are served together.

Fig. 25. A selection of cheeses: Caerphilly, Cheddar and Stilton.

It is at the table that the cheesemaker's art has its ultimate test. Few things so epitomise the traditions of the country table as the sight of a glass of ale or wine and a rich golden cheese with the distinctive aroma and taste that took hundreds of years to perfect.

8. Places to visit

Acton Scott
Wenlock Lodge, Acton Scott, Church Stretton, Salop (telephone: Marshbrook 322. Evenings: Church Streeton 2954).
Regular dairying demonstrations using milk from their farm.

Chewton Priory Farm Shop and Cheese Dairy
Chewton Mendip, Bath, Avon.
Cheesemaking on view to the public every day.

Easton Farm Park
Model Farm, Easton, Woodbridge, Suffolk (telephone: Wickham Market 746475).
A Victorian farm with a model dairy complete with a fountain ('coolness is the great requisite of the dairy'). This is a working farm.

James Countryside Museum
Bicton Gardens, East Budleigh, Devon (telephone: Budleigh Salterton 3881).
Agricultural museum which includes a large display of cheesemaking equipment.

Museum of East Anglian Life
Abbots Hall, Stowmarket, Suffolk (telephone: Stowmarket 2229).
Regular demonstrations of buttermaking and cheesemaking during the summer months at this partly open-air museum.

Museum of English Rural Life
University of Reading, Whiteknights, Reading (telephone: Reading 85123 extension 475).
Large library and records that may be consulted by appointment and a permanent exhibition of agricultural tools and implements from the nineteenth and twentieth centuries.

National Dairy Museum
Wellington Country Park, near Stratfield Saye, Reading (telephone: Heckfield 444).
The museum opened in 1978 and is situated at the entrance to the Wellington Country Park. It includes a replica of a Victorian farm dairy and examples of early equipment used in butter and cheese making and milk production.

Somerset Rural Life Museum
Abbey Barn, Glastonbury, Somerset (telephone: Glastonbury 32903).
Large display of dairy and cheesemaking equipment, including many historic items from the two-hundredth Royal Bath and West Show.

Wantage Museum
Civic Hall, Portway, Wantage, Oxfordshire (telephone: Wantage 66838).
Exhibits include a reconstructed dairy room with much of the equipment of the eighteenth and nineteenth centuries.

Equipment for the home cheesemaker
Clares Carlton Ltd, Wells, Somerset. Makers and suppliers of cheesemaking equipment to the trade.

Selfsufficiency and Smallholding Supplies, The Old Palace, Priory Road, Wells, Somerset (telephone: Wells 72127). Suppliers of equipment for the home cheesemaker; catalogue available.

Index